My Life as a Pioneer

Ann H. Matzke

rourkeeducationalmedia.com

Library of Congress EPCN Data

My Life as a Pioneer/Ann H. Matzke
(Little World Social Studies)
ISBN 978-1-61810-147-1 (hard cover)(alk. paper)
ISBN 978-1-61810-280-5 (soft cover)
Library of Congress Control Number: 2011945874

Rourke Educational Media
Printed in the United States of America,
North Mankato, Minnesota

Also Available as:

Educational Media

rourkeeducationalmedia.com

customerservice@rourkeeducationalmedia.com • PO Box 643328 Vero Beach, Florida 32964

Wagons Ho, **pioneers**! We say goodbye to friends and journey west to find a new home.

At Independence, Missouri, we join the **overland trail**.

PIONEER FACT

Towns near the start of the trail were called jumping-off places where pioneers bought wagons and supplies for the journey.

PIONEER FACT

Clothes, quilts, dishes, tools, lanterns, furniture, and 2,000 pounds (907.18 kg) of food were packed into a wagon.

We pack our supplies into a covered wagon called a **prairie schooner**. Four oxen pull our wagon.

With no room to ride inside the wagon, we walk along the trail ten to twenty miles (16.903 – 32.186 km) a day.

PIONEER FACT

It was a 2,000-mile (3,220 kilometer) journey across the United States and took five to six months to complete.

We see new animals along the trail, like **buffalo**. **Native Americans** sometimes help on our journey.

We travel all day. At sunset we stop to unpack the wagon, fetch water, and gather wood for a campfire.

13

After supper there is fiddle music, games, and stories to tell before we make our beds and fall asleep.

Bad weather, accidents, or illness can stop a wagon for days.

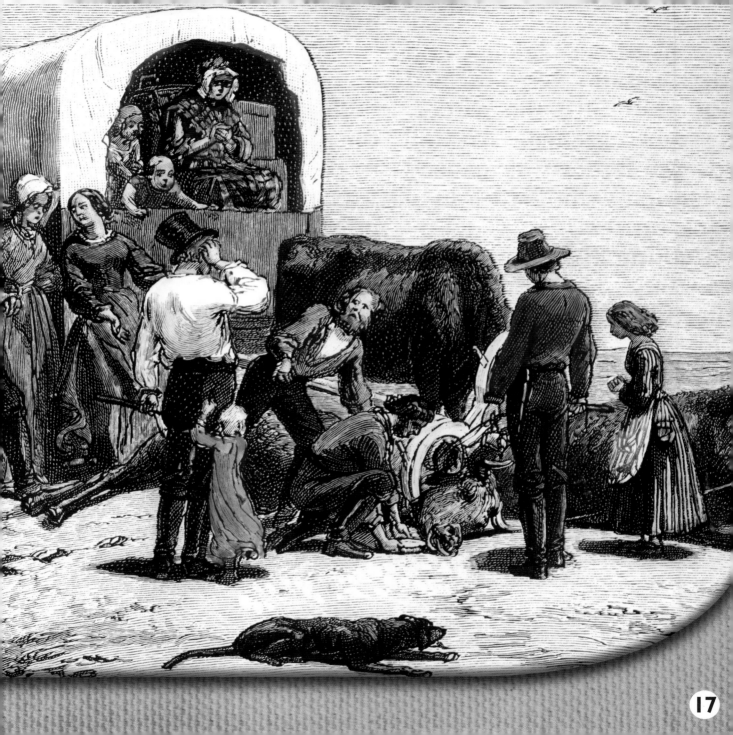

Landmarks guide our way.

After many hard months on the trail, we reach a new land ready to start a new life.

Picture Glossary

 **buffalo** (BUHF-uh-loh): An animal with thick fur and heavy horns, also called bison, that roamed the Great Plains in large herds.

 **landmarks** (LAND-marks): Objects in a landscape that can be seen from far away used to guide travelers.

 **Native Americans** (NAY-tiv uh-MER-uh-kuhns): The original people who lived in North America.